TEACHERS' RESOURCE

GUIDED AND INDEPENDENT READING

Introduction	3
A Suggested Teaching Sequence for Guided Reading	6
Selecting Texts for Guided Reading	7
Independent Reading	8
How to Get the Most Out of This Series	8
Evaluation and Monitoring	9
Glossary of Terms Used	10
The Titles	12
Teachers' Notes	14
Links to Themes	46
Links to Authors	53
Links to Illustrators	54
Index	55

• A balanced literacy program will include a wide range of reading and writing experiences, including reading **to** children, reading **with** children, and reading **by** children.

• The skills of literacy are developed, practiced and reinforced **in the context of actual reading**.

• Children should be exposed to a wide range of literature including:

— stories

— informational books

— traditional tales

— poetry

— plays

The teacher ensures that children meet with success as readers by:

• fostering and developing a love of books and helping children to see themselves as readers;

• providing time and many opportunities for reading;

• facilitating discussions that deepen children's understanding about books;

• fostering effective reading strategies;

• helping children to cope with challenges in text;

• giving encouragement and accepting approximations;

• matching the text to the abilities and interests of the children;

• providing many opportunities for rereading (e.g., reading to a friend, taking the book home to read to the family); and responding;

• continually observing and monitoring the ways in which children process print.

READING TO . . .

• Reading aloud **to** children provides many opportunities for them to hear stories they may not be able to read for themselves.

• It fosters a love and enthusiasm for reading.

• It enriches language development and provides many demonstrations of how language works.

READING WITH . . .

• Reading **with** children, or Shared Reading, encourages children to participate and become involved in the reading.

• The teacher's enthusiasm and presentation style demonstrate the joys of reading, and how stories work.

• It is a supportive approach that respects the children as co-readers. Repeated readings and time for responding help the children become confident to choose and read the text independently.

READING BY . . .

• Reading **by** children is the time when children take control of their own reading.

• This may take the form of independent reading where children choose to read and enjoy doing so. They choose from a variety of resources within the environment;

OR

• Guided Reading, where the teacher guides and supports the exploration of a book, trusting each reader to take increasing responsibility for the first reading of a text.

— Children who have reached similar stages of reading development work closely with the teacher in a small group of no more than eight.

— Each child is in the role of a reader, with his or her own copy of the selected book. The book will have been carefully chosen to be supportive, predictable, and closely matched to children's abilities,

needs and interests. The teacher involves the children in talking, reading and thinking their way through a story. In this way they come to know reading as a process of actively reconstructing meaning.

— The teacher acts as a facilitator; setting the scene, arousing interest, and engaging the children in discussion that will enable them to unfold the story line and feel confident and capable of reading the text for themselves.

— Approximations are accepted and rewarded.

— The teacher can closely observe and monitor the ways in which individual children process print.

• **Guided Reading is reading *by* children, but should the selected book prove to have too many challenges for the readers, making it difficult to understand, the teacher should read it with them as in Shared Reading.**

A SUGGESTED TEACHING SEQUENCE FOR GUIDED READING

1. Decide on the focus

• Know the children.

• What reading behaviors need to be practiced and consolidated?

• What reading behaviors need demonstration and development?

2. Select an appropriate book

• Know the book.

• Does it provide opportunities to build on the focus?

• Does it provide a manageable amount of challenge?

• Does it set specific purposes for reading?

• Does it require discussion throughout the reading?

• Does it have interest and appeal?

3. Set the scene

• Initiate discussion that will arouse interest in the book by referring to experiences in the children's own lives.

• Talk about the cover and title page, using open-ended questions that will stimulate ideas and help readers formulate their own purpose for reading.

• Read the title, author, illustrator.

• Ensuing discussion should continue to help children build anticipation of a story idea.

4. Read the text

• Having aroused interest and established in the readers a desire to take responsibility for controlling the first reading:

— Ask the children to read the text, intervening where appropriate to ask questions that carry the story line further and help them identify with the characters in a personal way;

— allow opportunity during the reading for children to discuss and ask their own questions of the author;

— ask "closed questions" where appropriate that encourage children to make predictions and read longer passages of text, in order to answer a question;

— let children reread the book independently or with a friend.

5. Return to the text

• Invite spontaneous response to the book.

• Encourage discussion in pairs on aspects of personal interest.

• Ask questions of the readers that encourage them to think more critically about the author's style, the mood, plot, theme, characters, etc.

• Reread the book, or parts of the book.

6. Respond to the text

• It is important to allow readers time to reflect on the experience.

• Responses will vary according to readers' interests and the opportunities provided to return to the story.

• Talk with the readers and have them talk with each other about the possibilities for responding.

• Demonstrate and facilitate creative responses that extend and complement the reading. Responses include: rereading, writing, arts and crafts, and dramatizing. A wide range of activities has been suggested.

• Encourage children to develop responses in pairs. Maintaining the creative interaction of all reading experience is important.

• Remember, it is not necessary to follow every story with an activity other than rereading for leisure and pleasure.

• Opportunities for extended creative involvement with a text extend and deepen a reader's view of himself or herself as a reader, writer, and illustrator.

• Provide the opportunity for children to share responses with the whole class if they wish. This develops oral language skills and social skills, and provides children with a genuine sense of audience and purpose. Sharing responses can be highly motivating and rewarding for the learner.

SELECTING TEXTS FOR GUIDED READING

Suitable texts for Guided Reading have meaning and appeal. They are supportive and predictable, and can be matched to the reader's level of development. They should have:

• high interest to motivate children to read with understanding;

• illustrations that enchance and support the text;

• enough challenge to let children practice and build on their existing language skills, while confirming their success as readers;

• natural language structures;

• supportive story structures such as rhyme, rhythm and repetition;

• repeated opportunities for children to meet the same words in many different contexts. This helps them develop their knowledge of high-frequency words, which are internalized and used naturally in writing.

INDEPENDENT READING

Independent reading is reading by children. It is when children choose to read, and enjoy reading for the pleasure of doing so. The teacher fosters independent reading by demonstrating and promoting it as a worthwhile activity at all times, and by showing genuine interest in the books that the children read.

Regular time must be allowed and a wide selection of stimulating books and other materials for easy reading made available to the children. These may include all forms of print found in a literate environment:

— books from book boxes, the book corner and the library;

— class magazines and newspapers;

— captions, labels and poem cards;

— published personal writing;

— published shared writing;

— charts, letters, invitations and organizational notices.

Independent reading is an integral part of the language program.

Lots of easy reading gives readers many opportunities to practice reading strategies and confirm their success as readers. In a rich literate classroom environment children at **all** levels of reading development should have opportunities for independent reading every day.

HOW TO GET THE MOST OUT OF THIS SERIES

The books in this series are designed as a flexible resource. Teachers are encouraged to draw on their knowledge

of the reading process and their understanding of the needs of individual children when choosing:

— which titles to read;

— the appropriate approach to use;

— what to focus on in reading and returning to the text.

To get the most out of the series, remember:

• Know each title well before introducing it to the children. Having a clear sense of the story line and the teaching and learning opportunities is essential when you come to setting the scene and talking the children through the story.

• The titles within each set can be used in any order. This freedom facilitates the closest possible matching of text to children's current needs, interests and experiences.

• The children's enjoyment and success as readers are paramount.

• The series is a rich resource of models and inspiration for children's writing. The input of reading has real impact on the output of writing.

• The books from Guided Reading

become favorites for independent reading, and form the basis for book boxes in which individual children accumulate personal stores of Books-That-I-Can-Read.

• Take advantage of the many opportunities that the books in the series provide for making links

— with the children's own experience;

— with authors' and illustrators' styles and techniques (a "Links to Authors and Illustrators" is provided at the back of this Teachers' Resource);

— with the themes (a "Links to Themes" section is provided at the back of this Teachers' Resource);

— across the curriculum.

• Be selective in using the ideas that the Teachers' Resource provides for each title, especially the activities for "responding to the text." These are starting points, not prescriptions. The aim is to show how, over a set of titles, a range of activities is possible and desirable.

EVALUATION AND MONITORING

Guided Reading is an ideal time for continual close observation of the ways in which individual children process print.

Below are some key points to consider in observing children's progress.

Do they:

• enjoy reading?

• expect the text to make sense?

• read to identify meaning rather than just identify words and letters?

• take risks and make sensible

predictions on the basis of meaning?

• self-correct when predictions are unsatisfactory?

• *When they come to a difficult word or phrase, do they:*

• read on to the end of the sentence?

• guess what the word might be?

• start again and read the whole sentence?

• use developing knowledge of letter-sound relationships to help?

• use developing word attack skills to help?

• predict what is to come in the text on the basis of an understanding of the story?

• predict, using their knowledge of how language works?

Eventually, children will come to use all of the above strategies.

Anecdotal notes provide a simple and effective way of recording your precise observations of reading behaviors. Reference to your analysis of these observations is essential in planning and preparing each Guided Reading lesson.

GLOSSARY OF TERMS USED

Anecdotal Notes

These are brief informal notes that record precise observations of behaviors, and shifts in behaviors, by individual children as they interact with their learning environment. These observations are ongoing, and provide valuable information about knowledge, skills and attitudes of each child.

Big Book

An enlargement of a book allows the whole class to join in reading a text they particularly enjoy. The enlargement of text allows the teacher to focus effectively on specific teaching points.

Brainstorm

Spontaneous discussion where thoughts and new ideas are shared and sometimes recorded on a chart.

Chart

A large sheet of tabulated or diagrammatic information.

• Time-line Chart
A time-line chart records a sequence of events. It gives children some conception of the passage of time. The time-line is divided into time blocks, for example:

— time during the day;
— seasons of the year;
— chronological time.

• Comparison Chart
Divide a large sheet of paper into two sections. Look at the different things you are comparing and list the differences on each side of the chart.

• Discussion Chart or Survey Results of discussions or class or group surveys are written on a large sheet of paper. The information can be used as a reference, as a guide, or as a basis for other creative activities; e.g., graphs.

• Class or Group Graph

To make a class graph, use a large sheet of paper or card and divide it into a grid. Make sure there is a column for each attribute you are looking at.

Flip-up Technique

This technique can be used in all the various methods for displaying enlarged text. Substitutions, answers to questions or innovations on text are written on additional strips or sheets of paper which are attached to a base display. The children lift the flaps to read the text.

Innovation

Using the text structure from a well-known story or rhyme, remake the story or rhyme substituting all or parts of the original text. The new version can reinforce and enrich vocabulary and sentence patterns featured in the original story. The children collaborate to produce the innovation, using their knowledge of the original story.

Story Map

This is an illustrated map of the action in a story. On a large sheet of paper, illustrate the setting; i.e., the scenery, homes, etc. Make the characters and place them on the map. Write labels, captions and speech bubbles for the map.

Wall Story

Children become physically involved with the text as they move along the wall, reading. The wall story is an effective way to use children's illustrations.

Zigzag Book

This book is made by joining pieces of heavy cardboard together with strong tape to form a fanfold reading resource which will stand up. Pictures and stories can be attached to the surface of the card.

STAGE FIVE TITLES

SET A

SET B

SET C

SET D

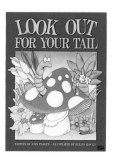

SET A

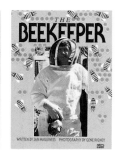

SET B

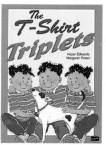

SET C

SET D

KNIT, KNIT, KNIT, KNIT

Setting the scene

- Discuss knitting with the children.
- Who has a knitter in the family?
- Who has friends who knit?

- Look at the cover together. Talk about the colored yarn. Predict the story. Look at the back cover. Discuss the colors and patterns in the sweater.

- Read the title, author, and illustrator.

Reading the text

- Talk about the title page.
- What are the two people doing?
- Are they friends?

- Support the reading of the text when necessary, discussing the pictures. Encourage the children to relate the picture and text to their own experience.

- Suggest the children read the text again independently. Be present for support.

Returning to the text

- Look through the pictures. Make a list of all the things Polly has knitted.

- Have the children reread the text independently, in the group; or with a friend.

- **Features to note in context:**

- Questions and answers. Discuss quotation marks and question marks. Talk about direct speech.

- Discuss silent *k* in *knit*. List other words children know where *k* is not sounded.

Responding to the text

- Look for other books about knitting (machine or hand).

- Provide yarn and needles and invite parents/school helpers into the classroom to assist the children in learning to knit.

Give a lot of support to the less able so that everyone succeeds.

- Suggest the children knit a scarf for their favorite doll or teddy bear to show to other classes.

- Ask them to wear their favorite knitted garment for their presentaton.

SOUVENIRS

Setting the scene

• Discuss with the children their experiences of souvenirs.

• Look at the cover. Talk about souvenir shops and what you find in them. Read the title, author and illustrator.

Reading the text

• Look at the title page and note the places to which the lady is planning to travel.

• Discuss the illustrations on each page; then ask the children to read the text. Offer support when needed.

Returning to the text

• Find a world map and read through the text again, finding all the places mentioned in the text.

— Ask for suggestions of other souvenirs that could come from those countries.

• Talk to the children about uppercase letters (capitals). Make a list of words from the text that start with a capital letter and discuss why.

Features to note in context:

— compound words: *double-decker,*

airport, windmill

Responding to the text

• Make a collection of souvenirs from places the children and teacher may have visited.

— Ask the children to label them as to where they were collected and why they were chosen.

— Divide the items into sets: (1) those collected by someone else and given to the children (2) those collected by the children for themselves (3) those collected by the children for someone else (4) those collected by someone else for themselves.

• Visit any local shops that sell souvenirs.

— Make a group book of your experience.

THE TICKLE-BUGS

Setting the scene

• Ask the children to share stories about occasions when they were sick. How did they feel? What parts of their bodies hurt? What did they do to help themselves get better?

• Read the title and discuss the cover illustration. Have the children guess what Tickle-Bugs are, utilizing just the cover illustration. Encourage them to articulate the reasons for their responses.

• Read the names of the author and illustrator.

Reading the text

• Turn to the title page. Is there further information found in the illustration to add to their earlier guesses about the Tickle-Bugs?

• Query the children about the illustration on pages 2 and 3. What is the object on the lower left-hand side? Guide the children to see that it's the same object that the boy is holding, yet magnified.

• Read the text on page 2 to familiarize the children with Andrew and his dilemma. Invite the children to read along with you.

• Generate questions as you talk through the story that help the children unfold the story line. For example:

— page 4: Who's making Andrew cough and sneeze?

— page 6: How do the Tickle-Bugs move their hairy little bodies? Can you find the part in the story that tells you? Does the illustration support the description of the Tickle-Bugs? How or why not?

— page 10: How did the Tickle-Bugs feel when Andrew covered his mouth? What do you think happened to them?

Returning to the text

• Suggest the children find a partner and take turns reading the Tickle-Bugs' song and conversations.

• Initiate a discussion that explores the concept of Tickle-Bugs. Ask: What do you think the author was trying to explain? Have you ever experienced Tickle-Bugs in your throat? What did you do to get rid of them?

• **Features to note in context:**

— contractions: *haven't, you're, we're, I've, we've, you've*

— number words: *two, thousand*

— punctuation: exclamation point

— homophones and homonyms: *to, two, too; flew, flue; drain, drain*

— double consonants: *happened, trapped*

— vocabulary that may need clarification: *tickle, flu*

Responding to the text

• Discuss and research ways to keep our bodies healthy. Explore the importance of a balanced diet, exercise, appropriate clothing, etc.

• Make Tickle-Bug puppets out of socks. Have the children bring in a sock and provide buttons and other fabric trimmings for the students to decorate their puppets. Suggest a puppet show presentation.

• Before reading page 16, make a last guess at what Tommy has in his hand.

Returning to the text

• Let the children reread the story again. Ask them to pay special attention to the questions the people asked, and consider these in relation to who the people were; e.g., the policewoman: *"Is it legal?"*

• **Features to note in context:**

— punctuation: direct speech

Responding to the text

• Ask the children to talk with each other about Tommy's magic spell.

• Look at page 16 and read again the list of words that describe the spell: *secret, valuable, interesting, beautiful, legal, surprising*. List these on a chart and ask the children to brainstorm other things that can be described by these words. There will be a lot of discussion.

• Discuss ways other people get attention. Are they always good ways?

• Suggest children use the adjective list on page 16 and work in pairs to re-create, write, and illustrate a new spell.

• Look at the beautiful colorful illustrations. Find pastels or crayons equally as bright and ask the children to illustrate their own surprising secret. (Ask them at the end if it is still a secret!)

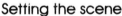

Setting the scene

• Ask the children what *treasure* means to them. List their ideas on a chart.

• Predict what Tommy's treasure might be. List predictions.

• What treasure could they have that they could hold in their hands?

• Ask the children to name a book they have read about treasure.

• Look at the front and back covers, and read the title.

Reading the text

• Read the title, author, illustrator, and title page.

• Read the text independently.

Setting the scene

• Have the children survey the cover illustration. Briefly discuss the detailed illustrations and then brainstorm possible story lines.

• Encourage the children to comment on possible settings, plots and types of characters they might find in this story. Have them support their ideas and predictions.

• Read the name of both the author and the illustrator.

Reading the text

• Read the title page together.

• The children will thoroughly enjoy reading this whimsical tale independently or with a partner. Its text and illustrations are very supportive.

• Demonstrate to the children how they can refer back to the illustrations to confirm their predictions about the story.

Returning to the text

• Allow time for a spontaneous discussion about the story. Which characters lured them into the story? Why? Elicit responses from the children about the structure of the story and the author's use of a rhyming text.

• Reread the parts of the story that described the animal's movement. Discuss the language used by the author to depict movement. How did the language impact the story's outcome?

• Explore and discuss figures of speech: *...hot on your trail, up like a rocket*

• Have fun with a choral reading of the story.

• **Features to note in context:**

– question words: *why, which, will*

– rhyming words: *Daniel - spaniel, ground - found*

– punctuation: dash, ellipsis

– suffix: *ing*

– vocabulary that may need clarification: *twitching, aglow, mynah, spaniel, stroll*

Responding to the text

• This is a delightful tale to dramatize. Suggest the children create a story map as a whole group prior to the reenactment. Explore setting, characters, problem, resolution.

• Create a word panel or chart that lists movement synonyms; e.g., *crouch: bow, dip, bend; leap: bounce, jump.*

DON'T WORRY

Setting the scene

• Elicit responses from the children about problem situations they've found themselves in. Have them share the ways in which they resolved their problem situations. Place emphasis on the process the children went through as they solved their problem.

• Survey the cover illustration. Encourage the children to make predictions about the story line. What information did they use to help them make their predictions?

• Read the title of the story, the author and the illustrator.

Reading the text

• Turn to the title page. Encourage the children to refine their predictions, based on any new information found in the illustration.

• Talk through the illustrations if appropriate to the needs of your children. Pose questions that encourage the children to go back to the text to support or confirm their responses; e.g.,

— page 2: What is the builder trying to do? Will it work? Why or why not?

— page 3: Find the text that tells why this idea didn't help the dog.

— page 10: What was the boy's idea? Do you think it will work? How do you think the dog feels about the idea?

— Have the children predict the story's outcome and then find the text that confirms their ideas.

— Enjoy reading this cumulative text with a friend, all together or alone. Provide support when needed.

Returning to the text

• Allow time for the children to spontaneously respond to the story.

Listen to the group's interaction and encourage the children to clarify their comments and reactions when appropriate.

• Lead a discussion on the problem-solving strategies used by the characters in the story. How would they respond to the dog's dilemma? Did they feel the boy's idea was the best solution to the problem? What about the idea generated in the end by the group? Would that be just as successful?

• Have the children read the story again.

• **Features to note in context:**

— suffixes: *er* and *ed*

— comma

— contractions: *don't, I'll, didn't, I'm*

— vocabulary that may need clarification: *rescue, mountain climber, carpenter*

Responding to the text

• Dramatize the story.

• Have the children brainstorm other creative solutions to help get the dog out of the well. Provide an assortment of materials (styrofoam pieces, wood, tubes, sticks, etc.) and have the children design a tool or a piece of equipment to get the dog out of the well.

• Locate other stories that have a similar story structure/plot. Compare and contrast the problems and resolutions found in the stories.

Setting the scene

• Ask the children what they do for fun. What things make them laugh?

• Look at the front and back cover illustrations. What kind of story might this be? What unusual things can be seen?

• Read the title, author, illustrator.

Reading the text

• Turn to the title page. What further predictions do the children make about the story?

• Pages 2 and 3: Ask the children what the characters are doing. Ask if anyone can read the words that the author uses to describe the pair.

• Read with the children, to get them into the structure of the text.

• Page 4: Refer to the characters and what they are doing. Then ask the children: What kind of threesome would that be? Ask what the word *gleesome* means.

• By pages 5-15, the children are likely to be familiar with the story structure, so continue to talk through the illustrations and aspects of the text as before, clarifying vocabulary where necessary.

• Page 16: Simply read all together; then suggest the children do as the author suggests, and read the rhyme again.

Returning to the text

• Ask the children to talk with the person beside them about features of the rhyme they find most interesting and/or funny.

• Return to the author's clever use of adjectives; e.g., *gruesome — twosome, gleesome — threesome*, etc., and talk about what the author's reasons might be for the choice of words.

• Discuss the words again, while

responding further to the illustrations.

• **Features to note in context:**

— compound words: look at the words ending in *some*. List them and make up more exciting words.

— punctuation: exclamation points

Responding to the text

• This story will likely generate many different responses from the children, from drama, to art, to innovations on the text structure. List the ideas that come from the children.

• There are many opportunities for demonstrating dictionary research.

• Remake the rhyme as a wall story or zigzag book.

• The children could make number sentences from the text; e.g., *3 storks and 2 flamingos equals a jivesome fivesome.*

Setting the scene

• Talk about the times the children have been ill. What was wrong, who looked after you, what did they do?

— What does having the measles look and feel like?

• Consider who might look after a dragon with measles.

Ask the children to draw from their book experience and talk about all the different characteristics a dragon might have.

• Read the title, author, and illustrator.

Reading the text

• Look at the title page. Read the title. How do you think the dragon is feeling?

• Read the first paragraph on page 3 out loud with the children (if you anticipate that the names of the characters might be too challenging for some of the readers) and let the children read on to the end of the page.

• Have the children read on through the text, discussing and responding to the illustrations on each page in the process.

• Ask questions that carry the story line forward.

• Page 15: Read the text. Comment on how everyone was happy. (Do the children notice Princess Petra is absent?) Ask them how they think the story will end.

• Read and respond to the final page.

Returning to the text

• Talk to a friend about the story.

• Ask the children to look in the text for the dragon's symptoms.

• Discuss how Petra and her helpers looked after the dragon.

— Why should he be kept warm?

— Why should he be kept out of the light?

— Why should he have lots to drink?

• Retell the story together through the illustrations.

Responding to the text

• Collect books about dragons and make a display under a dragon picture for the class to share.

• Suggest the children read *What Has Spots?* in Stage 2 of this series.

• With a friend, suggest the children write a set of instructions for someone who is caring for a friend with the measles. They may like to publish these on large cards (like a poem card) and display them for others to read. They could be called *Prescription Cards*.

Setting the scene

• Ask the children if they have ever wakened early in the morning and seen one little star still shining as the sun rises.

• It may be that some of the children know something about the morning star or the evening star. Invite them to share their knowledge.

• Look at the cover. What do the children notice about the illustration? Enjoy the fun shapes of the stars and the horizon.

• Ask the children to predict the genre; i.e., fact or fiction, and share ideas on why they may think it is one or the other.

• Read the title, author, illustrator.

Reading the text

• Turn to the title page, and ask the children to share further thoughts on what the story might be about.

• Read the text on page 2 together.

• On page 4, you might anticipate that the first sentence could be too challenging for some readers. Talk about waking — *yawning* — and what the *horizon* might be. Link directly to their own knowledge and experiences.

• Suggest the children read on independently within the group.

• Follow the procedure of anticipation and clarification where appropriate, as the children read through the story independently.

Returning to the text

• Ask the children to find parts of the text that tell them why
— the little star sighed
— the little star wanted to hide
— the moon was anxious

• **Features to note in context:**

— use of adjectives. List those found in the text and discuss alternatives.

Responding to the text

• Suggest the children retell the story to a friend and/or reread with a friend.

• Ask the children to help you make a list of adjectives. Let them choose their favorite one and dramatize it.

• Discuss the sky and talk about planets and stars. Observe what the children know.

• Go to the library and find out what happens when the earth goes around the sun.

• Make a chart of the earth's and moon's orbits. An interesting study could result.

• The children could act out the roles of the earth, sun, moon, and stars as depicted in the story.

THE SMALLEST TREE

Setting the scene

• Discuss the types of trees that are found in your schoolyard or nearby. Are there any particular trees that the children find interesting (seasonal, textures, size, leaves)? Encourage them to share any personal experiences relating to trees. For example, special climbing trees or possibly the building of a treehouse.

• Read the title, author and illustrator.

Reading the text

• Turn to the title page. Is there any additional information that can tell you about the story?

• Survey and discuss the illustrations on pages 2 and 3 to help the children establish the setting and possible story line.

• Read the text on page 2 to the children if appropriate. Encourage them to comment on the smallest tree's questions.

• Continue your way through the story by asking questions that draw the children's attention back to the text for clarification or confirmation.

Returning to the text

• Provide time for the children to talk about the story with a partner. Could they relate to the little tree's concern about being lonely or how he felt at the end of the story? Listen to their comments and use them to guide further inquiries about the group's reaction to the story.

• Read the story again and ask the children to find the part of the text in which the author gives the smallest tree human characteristics (personification).

• Have the children reread the text independently, with the group, or with a friend.

• Features to note in context :

— suffixes: *est, ing*

— use of a paragraph

— vocabulary that may need clarification: *autumn, evergreen*

Responding to the text

• Encourage children to use the author's technique of personification by having them imagine or write about an inanimate object, giving it human characteristics.

• If possible plant a tree with the class. Care for it and watch its growth.

• Compare and contrast evergreens and deciduous trees.

• Make spatter prints of leaves. Have the children collect an assortment of leaves. Provide construction paper, paint, toothbrushes and pieces of wire screens. (Make sure the edges are taped on the screens — 5" squares.) Have the children place the leaves on the paper and then rub the screen with a toothbrush dipped in paint. This should provide an outline of the leaves' shapes.

• Make a reverse print by having the children paint the backs of the leaves with paint — not too much. Place the paper on top of the leaves and use a roller to roll over the paper. Lift to see leaf print.

FRIENDS ARE FOREVER

Setting the scene

• Look at the front and back cover illustration and identify the animals.

— Discuss countries they can be found in and where you could find some of them in your nearest city.

— Would these animals ever all be found together? What would happen if they were all put together? Discuss the words *fact* and *fiction*.

• Read the title together. Ask the children to predict what the story might be about.

— Find out the children's definition of *friendship*.

— Look at the names of the author and illustrator.

Reading the text

• Turn to the title page.

— Observe the responses, if any, from the children.

— Talk about the possible relationship between the duck and the lion.

• Read page 2 together to support the children into the story line.

• Now suggest the children read on silently. The text is predictable and repetitive. Observe the readers closely and intervene with only enough questioning to ensure continuing understanding; e.g., page 6: What did Giraffe give Lion in return?

• Page 8: Ask: Why did Duck want to wear the crown? What did he have to offer Lion?

Returning to the text

• Suggest the children talk to the person beside them about the story.

• What are their thoughts on the title now?

• Talk about friendship again. Has the children's definition of friendship changed?

• Ask the children if there are any aspects of the story they wish to ask questions about.

— Reread the story with a friend.

• **Features to note in context:**

— punctuation: question marks

— page 8: why is NOT in uppercase?

— page 10: *SPLASH!* How should you read this?

Responding to the text

• Brainstorm the qualities of friendship and make a *Qualities of Friendship* chart.

• Make a *Friendship Book.* Children illustrate themselves with a friend, using wax crayons and/or bright dye. Children caption why that person (or animal) is a friend. Publish as a Big Book.

• Dramatize.

CAT CONCERT

Setting the scene

• Talk about cats and cat habits. Discuss the things cats might do at night.

• Look at the cover. Discuss what is happening. Ask the children to try and make the sounds of cats singing at night.

• Read the title, author and illustrator. Discuss concerts and the children's experiences of concerts.

• Ask the children why the author has chosen the title *Cat Concert*.

• What kind of story do you think it will be?

Reading the text

• Look at the title page.

— Discuss the picture. Allow time for the children to relate to the habits of their own cat; e.g., Is it put out each night or does it stay in with the family?

— Read the title.

• Read through the text, discussing the pictures before the verse on the page is read. Introduce words from the written text during the discussion.

• Ensure understanding of vocabulary in context.

Returning to the text

• Ask the children to share responses to the reading. What thoughts do they have about the author's style; i.e., use of

rhyme?

• Look through the text, finding words that describe the way the cats sing.

• Look at each verse and find the words that rhyme. Put the words in pairs and compare similarities and differences in spelling.

• Reread the text in pairs, singing the last in cat voices.

• **Features to note in context:**

— discuss *ow* as in *howl* and *show*

— words containing *ai* and *ay*

Responding to the text

• Collaborate to do a shared innovation on the story structure. You act as scribe on large pieces of newsprint. Children can illustrate in pairs. Make a Big Book.

• Collect cat books for a display. Include some cat poems among them. Read these to the children.

• Discuss the way Lyn Kriegler paints cats. Look at other cat illustrations.

• Brainstorm rhyming words that could be used for a cat poem or song.

— Put these on cardboard "bricks" or "planks" to form a "wall" on a dark-covered display board.

— Let the children make their own cat out of furry cloth to sit on the wall or fence.

— Write cat poems to scatter around the dark sky in the picture.

THE TWO FOOLISH CATS

Setting the scene

• Look at the front and back covers together. Ask the children to see if they can guess the location of the play.

• Locate Japan on the world map.

• Read the title, author, illustrator.

• Look at the word *Foolish*. Ask children to think of some foolish things that people do.

• Ask children to make predictions about the story from the title.

• Turn to the title page. Note the genre and reference to *Traditional*.

• Discuss the role of the narrator.

Reading the text

• Study the title page. Look at the three characters in the play. Suggest two children might read each character, and you take the part of the narrator, also reading the characters' instructions.

• Read page 2 all together to connect the children with the story line.

• On this first reading, you read the characters' instructions with expression.

• Support the readers as they meet with challenges in the text.

Returning to the text

• Invite the children to share their

responses to the play. What did they think of Mr. Monkey? Was there a lesson to be learned?

• Read the play again, this time with one child taking each character's part.

• Why were the cats *Foolish Cats*?

Responding to the text

• Present the play for the class, other classes, parents. Those who are not the characters can be playing instruments (when required) and the rest of the group can read the narrator's part (without the characters' instructions).

• Discuss a play production plan. Brainstorm ideas for the preparation; e.g.,

— Musical accompaniment. (What can be used to create an atmosphere?)

— Costumes. (Look at the illustrations together and plan making masks, tails and simple costumes.)

— Props. (List ideas for simple props.)

— Backdrop. (Research library for pictures of Japan and invite group participation to paint Japanese scenery.)

• After the play, have a class discussion on the message from the play.

• Approach a Japanese member of your community and discover how to make a rice cake. Alternatively, make a rice dish children enjoy.

HE WHO LISTENS

Setting the scene

• Spend time sharing titles of favorite folktales and discuss the features of a folktale that make it a literary genre.

• Survey the cover illustration. Inquire what the story might be about. Ask the children where they think the story may be set. Discuss what the old man might be doing in the illustration. Have the children support their responses, utilizing the illustration and personal experiences.

• Read the title. Let the children know that this particular story is an Eskimo folktale. Explore the children's knowledge of Eskimos. Provide information if necessary for their understanding of the story. Let their responses and insights guide the direction of your discussion.

• Read the author and illustrator.

Reading the text

• Turn to the title page. Does the illustration provide further information for the children to use to predict the story line?

• Before reading the story, take time to familiarize the children with unfamiliar concepts and vocabulary. Read relevant parts of the text to help the children visualize the Eskimo's quest and the underlying motive of the tale.

• If guiding the children through the story, make sure your questions lead the children back to the text to confirm their ideas about the story line. Here are just a few ideas:

— page 2: Why is the old man crouching on the ice?

— pages 6-9: What did the children do to make the old man so angry? Why did it bother him? What was the outcome of his anger?

— pages 10/11: Why did the old man run away from the people? How do you think he felt when he saw them coming?

Returning to the text

• Spend time discussing the story's setting. Bring attention to the clothes, physical environment, animals, etc. Talk about the man's reaction to the children and consequence of his actions. Explore the children's feelings about the end of the story. Elicit responses from them about their feelings for the man and the children.

• The children will be fascinated with the Eskimo's explanation of how Venus, the morning star, came to the night sky. Provide the opportunity for them to react to this phenomenon.

• Marie Low's illustrative style is quite distinct. Spend time discussing her illustrations and how the details support the essence of the story.

• Have the children read the story together, with a friend, or by themselves.

• **Features to note in context:**
— suffixes: *ed, ing, less*
— blends: *cl, cr*
— double vowels: *ea, ee*

Responding to the text

• Have the children find, locate and share via booktalks other stories/folktales that explain natural phenomena (see esp. Native American folktales).

THE BEEKEEPER

Setting the scene

• Discuss the cover with the children.

— What kind of job does the man have?

— Is it dangerous?

— Have you been stung by a bee? What does it feel like? Are you allergic to bee stings?

— What happens to a bee when it stings?

— Why do people keep bees?

• Read the title, author, illustrator.

Reading the text

• Look at the title page. Read the title.

— Discuss the hexagonal shapes and what they might be used for.

— Decide what "family" the bees belong to (insects). How many legs do they have and how are their bodies constructed?

• Read the text together, discussing the photographs and encouraging anecdotal comments.

Returning to the text

• Let the children read with a friend.

• Discuss words that don't appear in the text but do in mathematics; e.g., *hexagon* and *tessellate*.

• Make a list of interesting words that do appear in the text.

• **Features to note in context:**

— use of a glossary

— punctuation: colon

Responding to the text

• Research: Go to the library with the group and use the catalog, looking under *Bees* and *Insects*.

• Demonstrate note taking and show the children how to find important information in the text of the books they find.

• Collect and make a display of books about bees.

• Make a big chart of the information that the children have found about bees.

• Mathematics: Tessellate hexagon shapes to make patterns. Turn them into colorful pictures. Experiment to find what other shapes can tessellate.

• Invite a beekeeper to school. Ask him to bring the clothes he wears when he works with his bees. The children could have a list of questions to ask him. Show him the information chart that the children have made. Ask him to respond to our findings.

• Make a thank you card for the beekeeper out of tessellated shapes.

• Taste some raw honey. Then cook with honey. Look up favorite recipes and let the children decide what they would like to make.

• Alternatively, make Honey Sauce and serve with ice cream.

1/4 cup apple juice   1/4 cup chopped walnuts
1/4 cup raisins   1 cup honey
2 tablespoons butter

— Put apple juice and raisins in a small saucepan and let stand for 10 minutes to swell raisins.

— Add butter, walnuts, and honey to saucepan and cook for 10 minutes, stirring constantly.

— Take off the heat, and cool slightly.

— Serve warm over vanilla ice cream.

• Now read *Diary of a Honeybee*.

DIARY OF A HONEYBEE

Setting the scene

• Recall *The Beekeeper*. Read *The Beekeeper* again.

• Read *Caterpillar Diary* by David Drew (RIGBY, Stage 2).

• Discuss the word *diary*.

Reading the text

• Read the title page together and discuss the picture. Who would be writing the diary?

• Read the text, discussing the photographs as you read.

Returning to the text

• Reread the text until page 16. Look at the words in the *Glossary* and discuss them.

• Features to note in context:

— sentence construction: look for nouns and verbs in the text

— use of a glossary

— diary format

Responding to the text

• Find lots of different diaries. See how they are set out.

• Ask the children to think of a diary they could keep on a topic (e.g., growing a bean).

• Look at page 15. Add to this list of facts. See how many more the children can add to a chart. (Perhaps the chart you made for *The Beekeeper*.)

• Get some pollen and nectar from a flower. Look at them under a microscope. Ask the children to talk about and record their observations. Does the experience raise more questions for them?

• Library research: Go to the library. Assist the children to discover how plants are pollinated by bees. (Try growing beans in the classroom and do the bees' job of pollination.) Discover how many other ways plants are pollinated.

• Using papier-mâché or clay, suggest the children make a model of a bee. When it is dry, paint the bee the correct colors. When it is completed, they can label the parts of the bee and explain what they are used for.

THE LONELY GIANT

Setting the scene

• Look at the cover illustration. Read the title.

• Ask questions such as: What does lonely mean? Have you ever felt lonely? When and why? Who do you think might live in the house shown on the cover? How do you know it isn't the giant's house?

• Discuss briefly whether the children have read other stories by this author and illustrator.

Reading the text

• Read the title page together.

• Read children pages 2 and 3. Discuss the scene, and encourage further predictions about the story. Ask questions such as: What kind of people do you think the old woman and the giant might be? (Look at the illustrations on pages 2 and 3 for clues.) How do you think the giant feels about the old woman? Why? What do you think might happen?

• Talk through the illustrations up to page 16. Read selected parts of the text, focusing on the vocabulary: *puzzled, thrust, great*.

• Children read the text independently up to page 16. Discuss. List their predictions for the rest of the story. Read to the end as a group, and compare the story with the prediction list.

• Read the story together, with children clapping on the *clickety clack*.

• Have the children reread the text independently, with the group, or with a friend.

Returning to the text

• Note the use of colored type. Then have the children read the story in groups of three, one person to narrate, the others to read the dialogue of the old woman and the giant.

• Discuss the story: Why was the giant lonely? Do you think the old woman was lonely? What kind of a person was the old woman? (Look at what she does and says.) How does the old woman make friends with the giant?

• **Features to note in context:**

— bold print to show emphasis

— spelling: double letters — *puzzled, suddenly, bigger, knitting, woolly*

— soft *g: giant*

Responding to the text

• Make a list of the attributes children think friends should have.

• Write similes about friendship; e.g., *A friend is like a warm woolly scarf on a cold day.*

• Teach children to knit a simple scarf on big needles.

• In pairs write scripts based on the story. Dramatize them.

• Write thank-you letters from the giant and the old woman to each other. How might they each say thank you? Would their letters sound the same?

• Paint the wintry scene where the story takes place, using cold colors.

Setting the scene

• Look at the front and back covers of the book. Read the title.

• Ask questions such as: What could the words "Oogly Gum" mean? Who do you think the characters in the illustrations are? How do you expect this story to make you feel? Is this a modern or an old-fashioned story? How do you know? Is it realistic or imaginary? Why?

• Briefly discuss whether the children have read other stories by this author or illustrator.

Reading the text

• Read the title page together.

• Read pages 2 and 3 with the group and encourage further predictions.

• This story is modeled on the pattern of many traditional stories. It has three episodes (pages 4–7; pages 8–11; pages 12–23), and a happy ending. Have the children read each episode individually or in pairs (after discussing the illustrations if support is necessary). Stop at the end of each episode, so the group can make predictions about what might follow.

• When children have finished the story,

read it through together.

Returning to the text

• Provide opportunities for children to reread the story for pleasure.

• Discuss the story: How would you describe the dragon in the story? What parts of the story did you like best? Is this a realistic or imaginary story? How is the little girl like girls you know? How is she different? How is she different from the other characters in the story?

• Features to note in context:

— rhyming and onomatopoeic words: *oozy goozy* (Find the meaning of *oozy* in the dictionary.)

— alliteration: *great green*

— hyphenated names: *Sir Bounce-a-lot; Sir Boast-a-lot*

Responding to the text

• Write a more mysterious title for the story.

• Make a collection of onomatopoeic words, such as *oozy goozy*.

• Read other books about dragons; e.g., *Lucy Meets a Dragon* by Susan Reid, Literacy 2000, Stage 5; *Dragons*, RIGBY Informational Books, Stage 7.

• Make a collage of the oozy goozy swamp and the dragon.

• Create music with percussion to accompany the dragon's chant.

THE PUMPKIN HOUSE

Setting the scene

• Before asking the children to look at the cover, ask: Who might live in a pumpkin house?

• Look at the cover and ask questions such as: Why might a pumpkin house be good for a mouse? If you could have a new house, what kind would you have? Would you make a house out of a pumpkin? Why? Why not?

Reading the text

• Read the title page together.

• The illustrations give a lot of support to the text in this story. Depending on the needs of the children, allow them to read the story alone or in pairs. Offer assistance if necessary.

• Read the whole story together.

Returning to the text

• Talk about the story.

• Reread the story.

• Discuss: What other edible houses have you read about? (e.g. the witch's house in *Hansel and Gretel*, the peach in Roald Dahl's *James and the Giant Peach*) If you could have an edible house, what kind would you have? What words would you use to describe this story? (e.g. *funny, silly, yummy, imaginary*) What words would you use to describe Flora? (e.g. *busy, clever, hungry*) What does the question at the end of the story make us expect?

• **Features to note in context:**

— the repetitive structure of the text as a basis for innovation

Responding to the text

• Make a model of Flora and her house, using junk material and a pumpkin.

— Display the steps taken to make a pumpkin house.

• Write the end of the story on a class chart of interesting story endings.

• Make things with vegetables; e.g., a cucumber bus with sliced-carrot wheels. (See *Look What I Made!* RIGBY, Literacy 2000, Stage 2)

• Make a chart about the houses and needs of different animals.

• Find a recipe for one of the foods that Flora eats, such as pumpkin pie.

— Write the recipe on a chart.

— Talk about the different parts of a recipe; e.g., ingredients, method.

— Follow the recipe as a class cooking activity.

• Rewrite the events in the story as Flora's diary.

ALISON WENDLEBURY

Setting the scene

• List the stories children can think of that have someone's name as the title. Talk about what the stories were like.

• Look at the cover illustration and read the title.

• Ask questions such as: What will a story called Alison Wendlebury be about? Who will be the main character? Why are there two girls on the cover?

Reading the text

• Read the title page together.

• Read pages 2 and 3. What further predictions do children have?

• The strength of this story is in the deep feelings expressed through simple language. Allow children time to read it for themselves. Offer support where needed.

Returning to the text

• Talk about the story.

• Reread the story.

• Discuss: How do you feel about each of the characters? Find a page in the story where you know how the narrator feels. Who do you think is the best friend of all? How does the narrator show Alison how she feels? Do you think this was a good idea? Why don't you think the narrator (the I) has a name? What do you think the end of the story means?

• Feature to note in context:

— punctuation: dash (pages 9 and 24)

Responding to the text

• Have children work in pairs to write. Provide models of types of writing before they begin:

— Write an advertisement for a friend, including the qualities required.

— Write a diary for the main character of

the events in the story.

— Rewrite the story using boys' names and activities.

— Make a "wanted" poster for a friend.

— Work in pairs to write a script based on the story.

Share the writing with the group and discuss whether the results have the same feelings as the story. OR

• Read an episode from the story, while pairs of children mime the feelings of the characters:

— Give them paper bags or masks to cover their faces, so that they can use body language only.

— Have them kneel behind a table so they can use facial expressions only.

— Discuss their impressions of these two different forms of mime.

MR. PEPPERPOT'S PET

Setting the scene

• Talk about pets and taking them to the vet.

• Show children the cover illustration and title.

• Ask questions such as: What do you think Mr. Pepperpot's pet might be? What kind of pet do you carry in a sack? What might happen to a mysterious pet? Is this going to be a realistic or an imaginary story? Why?

• Briefly discuss whether the children have read any stories by this author or illustrator.

Reading the text

• Read the title page together. Make further predictions.

• Talk through the illustrations up to page 15, reading the sign on page 2 and the names of the characters. Note the containers held by each character and encourage prediction about what might be inside.

• Individually or in pairs, have children read the story, stopping at the end of the following pages to make further predictions: page 15; page 23.

• Read the story right through, as a group, in pairs or individually.

Returning to the text

• Provide opportunities for children to reread the story for pleasure.

• Discuss the story: How did you feel when you didn't know what the pets were? What effect does Mr. Pepperpot's pet have on the other pets? What is a *chain reaction*? Which pet starts the chain reaction and the noise? How does everyone feel on the last page? Why? Which page do you like best? Why? Do you think the illustrations show the events clearly?

• **Features to note in context:**
— possessive apostrophe: *Mr. Pepperpot's Pet*, etc.

— alliteration: *Mrs. Fooglegum's Frog; lizard leaped; tortoise tumbled*

Responding to the text

• Use the story as a model for a class story involving Mr. Pepperpot's python in another situation; e.g., at a bus stop.

• Look at how the illustrator has shown movement in her illustrations. Have children choose a page they would like to illustrate in their own way.

• Make a recording of this story, with some children narrating and playing the characters, and others making the sound effects of the animals.

• Read other "chain-reaction" stories to compare with *Mr. Pepperpot's Pet*.

SOMETHING SOFT FOR DANNY BEAR

Setting the scene

• Look at the cover illustration and read the title.

• Ask questions such as: What might the something soft be? Why might Danny Bear get something soft? What is happening in the cover picture? Do you think this is a realistic or an imaginary story? Why?

• Briefly discuss whether children have read other books by this author or illustrator.

Reading the text

• Read the title page and make further predictions about the characters in the story.

• Suggest the children read the story alone, one section at a time. Stop at the end of the following pages to discuss what has happened and what might happen next: page 11, page 13, page 15, page 21, page 23.

Returning to the text

• Provide time for everyone to read the story right through again.

• Ask children to find particular parts of the story; e.g., where Danny and Blackie find the couch. What happens before that? What happens after?

• Discuss the story: How are the bears in the story like real bears? How are they like imaginary bears? What event makes the whole story happen? Find that part. Who are the main characters? Why is Blackie a good friend?

• **Features to note in context:**

– questions and question marks

– alliteration (page 10)

Have the children reread the text independently, with the group, or

with a friend.

Responding to the text

• Dramatize the conversations between Danny and Blackie. How would they talk?

• Write class report cards for Danny or Blackie. What are their good and bad points?

• Write similes: *As soft as...*

• Research the hibernation patterns of bears.

• Make a model of Danny's house, inside a box. Use junk material for the furniture and cardboard cutouts for the characters. Make viewing slits in the roof, but cover them with dark cellophane to keep it like a cave.

• This story is about recycling. Talk about the importance of this for the future of the earth. How can each person recycle things at home?

THE T-SHIRT TRIPLETS

Setting the scene

• Look at the cover illustrations and have them predict what the story might be about. Read the title.

• Ask questions such as: What do you know about triplets or twins? Could this be a realistic or imaginary story? Why?

• Discuss briefly whether children have read stories by this author or illustrator.

Reading the text

• Read the title page together.

• This story is a series of episodes. Before reading the whole story, allocate different children just one episode each to read alone.

• Bring the group together to discuss what they think of the characters, and what they expect to happen in the rest of the story. Encourage individuals to show an illustration or read out part of the text to explain what they think.

• Have children read the whole story independently.

Returning to the text

• Provide many opportunities for rereading the story for pleasure.

• Discuss the story: Why don't the triplets mind if everyone gets them mixed up? How do you think the triplets feel about each other? When is it fun to pretend to be someone else? How does the illustration help us to understand the last page?

• **Features to note in context:**

— punctuation: direct speech

— hyphenated words: *mix-up; T-shirt*

Responding to the text

• Divide the story into chapters. Write a new title for each chapter.

• Write a new episode about the triplets.

• Look at the different arrangements of the triplets in the illustrations in the story.

— Make different patterns out of groups of three paper shapes, e.g. three triangles, three squares, three circles.

• Multiply things by three: e.g., If the triplets have two sandwiches each, how many sandwiches altogether? How many shoes do triplets wear?

• Invite a parent of twins to talk about looking after more than one baby.

• Let children print their names on a T-shirt or pocket, using batik, potato printing, screen printing, spatter painting over a stencil, or appliqué.

THE LITTLE GIRL AND HER BEETLE

Setting the scene

• Look at the cover illustration.

• Ask questions such as: Who do you think the little girl might be? What might she do with the beetle? Have you ever had a beetle? What did you do with it? Do you think this will be a realistic or imaginary story?

• Read the title.

Reading the text

• Read the title page together and make further predictions from the illustration.

• Read page 2 and ask what might happen.

• Talk through the illustrations up to the end of page 15, and read the last line on each page, encouraging further predictions. Have children read the story in pairs up to page 15. Discuss their predictions for the rest of the story. Read to the end in pairs.

Returning to the text

• Reread the story, with children reading the cumulative parts on each page.

• Within the group, retell the events of the story in sequence.

• Discuss the story: Who is the main character? Who are all the other characters? How are they important? What does the little girl do to get everything started? Why does the little girl let the beetle go?

• Features to note in context:

— capital letters for names

— contraction: *won't*

Responding to the text

• In pairs, write the events on separate cards for a sequencing activity.

• Innovate on the pattern of this story to make a new class Big Book.

• Write the story on a wall chart, using the children's illustrations.

• Collect beetles and observe them. (Use *Creature Features*, RIGBY Informazing, as a reference.) Record observations.

-- Make a chart of their different features.

— Let them go when the information is collected.

• Read other stories or rhymes with a similar pattern; e.g., *The Old Woman and the Pig* (Mother Goose), *A Silly Old Story*, by Joy Cowley, RIGBY Read-alongs, Stage 5.

DOGSTAR

Setting the scene

• Look at the title and ask if anyone can read it.

• Ask questions such as: What do you think the word *Dogstar* means? Is it a real word? Is it a name? Does the title seem to match the cover illustration? In what way? Who can suggest what's happening in the illustration and why?

• Briefly discuss whether children have read other stories by this author or illustrator.

Reading the text

• Read the title page together.

• Talk through the illustrations and text before the children read the story alone or in pairs. Alternatively, read the story with the children, demonstrating strategies for decoding unknown words. Ask them to note new words that we could find out more about. List these as you share. Suitable words:

mongrel, musician (page 2); *station* (page 3); *especially* (page 4); *tomorrow* (page 10); *steak* (page 11); *delicious* (page 12); *performance* (page 13); *safety* (page 15); *laughed, wheelies* (page 17); *guest* (page 19); *photographs, autographs* (page 22); *agent* (page 23).

• Children read the story right through.

Returning to the text

• Suggest the children talk with a friend about the text.

• Discuss: Who is telling the story? How does "Muddy the Mongrel" become "Dogstar"? (List the events in sequence.) What kind of musician is Tom? (Find sentences which show this.) Is this a realistic or imaginary story? Why? How do Tom and Dogstar feel about each other? (Find sentences which show this.)

• **Features to note in context:**

— compound words - *dogstar, railway, something, skateboard, pawprint*

— hyphenated words: *one-man, thank-you* (adj), *sound-proof*

• Reread all or parts of the story.

Responding to the text

• In pairs, write the main events of the story on separate cards.

— Illustrate and use for a sequencing activity.

• Rewrite the events in the story as Dogstar's diary.

• Make a poster advertising Dogstar's next show.

• Start a class autograph book for visitors to sign.

• Create instruments that can be played together as a one-man band.

THE SKELETON ON THE BUS

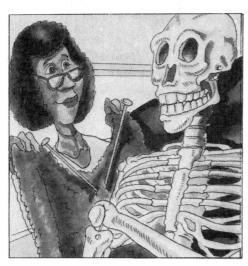

Setting the scene

• Show children the cover and title, so they can make predictions.

• Ask questions such as: What kind of story do you expect this to be? (Scary? Funny?) Why? Will it be realistic or imaginary? Why?

• Brainstorm a list of things that children think could happen when a skeleton gets on a bus.

Reading the text

• Read the title page together.

• Talk through the illustrations, before children read the story alone or in pairs. Alternatively, before reading, copy heavily-cued paragraphs from the story onto separate pieces of paper (e.g., page 5; para 1 page 9; para 1 page 12; page 15; page 18; page 20). Give each child or pair a paragraph, allowing time for reading and rereading, and providing support if necessary. Read the story to the children, stopping before each chosen paragraph. The child who thinks he/she has the missing paragraph reads it out. Discuss

with the group whether it "fits" the story so far.

• Children reread the story in pairs or small groups.

Returning to the text

• Provide opportunities for children to reread the text for pleasure.

• Discuss the story: What makes this story funny? When do you know that this isn't going to be a scary story? Why? Which is your favorite part? Why? What is clever about the driver's words on the last page?

• **Features to note in context:**

— punctuation: *quotation marks, exclamation points*

— spelling - doubling letters: *shop — shopping, knit — knitting, grab — grabbed*; double letters: *poodle, feed, sleeve, lettuce, nibble, opposite*

Responding to the text

• Use the dialogue in the story for a comic strip or play script.

• Make book posters about the story. Use an illustration and a short description to attract a reader, but don't tell everything.

• Find out about skeletons. Use *Body Maps* (RIGBY *Informazing*) as a reference.

• Do a skeleton dance to music, such as the *Dans Macabre* by Saint Saens.

DOM'S HANDPLANT

Setting the scene

• Discuss the title of the book. Who might Dom be? What is a handplant?

• Discuss the cover and ask further questions to encourage prediction: What do you expect from a book with photographs instead of illustrations?

• Draw children's attention to the words *photographed by*.

Reading the text

• Read the title page together.
• Read the text individually, in pairs or as a group.

Returning to the text

• Allow opportunities for children to reread the story for pleasure.

• Discuss the story: What is the problem with the first skateboard ramp? Why can't Dom do a handplant at the beginning of the story? How does Dom do something about getting a ramp in the park near his home? How does Dom find out that a new ramp will be built? Why can Dom do a handplant at the end of the story? How has the author made the story exciting?

• Have groups of children write the main events of the story in sequence.

• **Features to note in context:**
-- The language and layout of letters and newspaper articles

-- Punctuation: ellipsis (pages 7 and 23); commas in a list (page 14); quotation marks; possessive apostrophe *Dom's handplant, mayor's hand*

Responding to the text

• Use the book as a model and stimulus for children's writing; e.g.,

— Write a letter to the mayor about a local problem.

— Write a newspaper article about a current event in the school. Try to have it published by the local paper.

• Talk about setting and achieving goals through practice and commitment.

• Use the design of the book as a stimulus for children's own publishing.

• The children could work in small groups to write a simple story, planning photographs as they go. Photograph the events and publish the finished books.

• Role-play a mayor's meeting.

— Divide the class into two groups: the local citizens and the children.

— Have each group prepare arguments for or against a skateboard ramp.

— Have each group choose a speaker to present their arguments at the meeting.

LUCY MEETS A DRAGON

Setting the scene

• Before giving the children the book, ask questions such as: What would you do if you met something scary? How do dragons in stories behave?

• Show them the title and cover illustration and ask questions such as:

What kind of dragon do you think this story is about? Who do you expect Lucy to be? What do you think she'll do when she meets the dragon? (Make a list of the possible characteristics of Lucy and the dragon.) Do you think this is an imaginary or a realistic story? Why?

Reading the text

• Read the title page together.

• Talk through the illustrations in segments, stopping to allow children to read each segment and then predict the next segment with the group. Suitable prediction points are at the end of pages: 3, 7, 9, 11, 15, 19, 20, and 21. (Choose the number of prediction points depending on the amount of support the children need.)

• Read the whole story through again, individually, in pairs or as a group.

Returning to the text

• Provide opportunities for children to return to the text for pleasure.

• Discuss: How do you think Lucy feels about her new house? How does she first feel about the dragon? When do her feelings change and why? Is this a realistic or an imaginary story (or a little of both)?

• **Features to note in context:**
— adding *ing* to different root verbs: *run — running; tickle — tickling*
— sentence structure (using a sentence as a model): *Out spilled silk/in all the colors of the rainbow.* (page 4) *Up jumped Jack/in a brightly striped suit.*

Responding to the text

• Have a class "Chinese" dragon parade.

— Use a decorated carton for the head, and crepe paper for the body.

• Find out about Chinese dragons, and the Chinese people and their culture.

• Collect stories about dragons; e.g., *Pete's Story*, Literacy 2000, Stage 6.

• Make a dragon dictionary, with details and illustrations from each story.

• Paint a dragon mask. Show whether the dragon is fierce or friendly.

• Read other stories about moving house; e.g., *Rosie's House*, also by Susan Reid, Literacy 2000, Stage 6.

ZOE AT THE FANCY DRESS BALL

Setting the scene

• Read the title and look at the cover illustration.

• Discuss briefly whether the children have read other stories by this author or illustrator.

• Ask questions such as: What happens at a fancy dress ball? What do you think Zoe dresses as? What might happen to a fairy at a ball? Will this be a realistic or an imaginary story?

Reading the text

• Read the title page together.

• Talk through the illustrations before children read the story alone or in pairs. Alternatively, before looking at the story, have the main events written on separate cards. Read them with the children and help them sequence the events in a possible story sequence. Discuss alternatives. A suggested list ready for sequencing: Zoe isn't happy with the costume./Her mother and father make her a costume./Zoe can't decide what to wear to the fancy dress ball./Everyone cheers Zoe for being a magic fairy./At the ball the lights go out./Zoe is given a prize for helping the judge./On the day of the ball Zoe decides to be a fairy./Suddenly the lights come back on.

• After the sequencing, children read the story alone or in pairs. Compare the sequenced events with the story.

Returning to the text

• In pairs or trios, let the children talk about the parts of the story they enjoyed reading most.

• Discuss the story: Is this realistic or imaginary (or a little of both)? Which part is magical? Why isn't Zoe happy about her costume? What could she have done about it? What is said on page 8 that turns out to be special? What makes Zoe feel like a real fairy on page 23? What would you do with the last wish?

• **Features to note in context:**
— punctuation: dash (page 6); ellipsis (page 13); commas (page 22); exclamation points

Responding to the text

• Write the beginning of this story on a chart of interesting beginnings.

• Dress cutout figures from magazines in fancy dress, using collage.

• Have each child write a new ending for the story. Share them.

• Have a class fancy dress ball. Create part of the costumes at school; e.g., masks, hats, props.

• Write a report card for Zoe, showing her strengths.

• Read other stories that contain three wishes, such as traditional stories; e.g., *The Three Wishes*.

Setting the scene

• Discuss the title and cover illustration. Point out the words *Retold by* and discuss what children already know about traditional stories.

• Ask questions such as: Have you heard a story with this title before? What was it about? Do you think this is the same story? Why? What might be different about this story? If children don't know the story, ask: What kinds of characteristics might a hare and a tortoise have? What might happen to them?

• If appropriate, talk about fables and the elements they contain.

Reading the text

• To recapture some of the oral tradition of this story, read it aloud or tell your own version to the children before they have their own copy. Use strong character voices and facial expressions.

• Give children their own copies to read alone or with a partner.

Returning to the text

• Provide opportunities for children to reread the story for pleasure.

• Discuss the story: What kinds of characters are Harry Hare and Tommy Tortoise? (Find examples in the story.) Why do you think this story uses animals instead of people? How do a hare and a tortoise suit the story? What is the story trying to teach us?

• **Features to note in context:**

— new vocabulary: *challenge, boasting, appeared*

— punctuation: *ellipsis* (page 23)

— rhymes: *ready/steady; eyes/surprise; face/place*

Responding to the text

• Talk about fables:

— Read other versions of this fable and other fables.

— Have children prepare a retelling of a fable. Try it out in pairs.

• Choose an issue of importance to the class.

— Have children work in groups to create their own fable about the issue.

— Remind them to use animal characters and a brief telling.

— Record their fables on tape for publishing in a class book of *Fables*.

MATTHEW'S TANTRUM

Setting the scene

• Look at the cover illustration and read the title.

• Ask questions such as: What is a tantrum? Who usually throws tantrums? How old do you think Matthew is? Why might Matthew throw a tantrum?

• Encourage children to share their own experiences of tantrums.

• Briefly discuss whether children remember other stories by this author or illustrator.

Reading the text

• Read the title page and pages 2 and 3. What other predictions can be made?

• Talk through the illustrations, and read only the dialogue on each page to prepare children for their own reading. Leave out the last page.

• Before children read, pose a question for them to focus on while reading: What feelings make Matthew throw a tantrum?

• Children read the story alone or in pairs.

• Discuss their answers to the question.

Returning to the text

• Allow children time to reread the text for pleasure.

• Discuss the story: Who is telling the story? How does Timmy feel about his little brother? When does Matthew's mother expect trouble? What event makes Matthew throw a tantrum? How does Matthew's mother help him get over it? Why does she tell Timmy he can't throw a tantrum? What does the last illustration tell us?

• **Features to note in context:**

— pronouns: *I, my, he* (pages 2/3 and 22/23)

— punctuation: commas (pages 13 and 19); ellipsis (page 13); possessive apostrophe: Matthew's Tantrum

• Have the children reread the text independently, with the group, or with a friend.

Responding to the text

• Talk about ways of being angry that don't hurt anyone.

— Make a zigzag book. *When I'm angry I...*

When I'm angry I... turn red in the face
clench my fists
yell at the clouds

• Talk about children's own experiences with little brothers or sisters.

• Read other stories about similar feelings; e.g., *The Frown* by Janet Slater Redhead, RIGBY Read-alongs Stage 4.

• Do an illustration for page 2, showing how Timmy feels about his brother.

• Collect children's baby photos for a class book about growing up.

— Write captions that focus on the stages of development.

• Look at the illustration on pages 14 and 15. Paint masks of angry faces.

• In small groups, write the main events in the story on separate cards.

— Illustrate and use for a sequencing activity.

CAMPING WITH CLAUDINE

Setting the scene

• Look at the cover illustration and title.

• Ask questions such as: What do you expect the camping trip to be like? What kind of campers do you think the characters are? What is happening in the cover picture? Is this a realistic or an imaginary story? Why?

• Briefly discuss any stories by this author or illustrator which the children may know.

Reading the text

• Read the title page and page 2. Ask: What do you think the characters are like? How do you expect the story to be written? What might happen?

• Depending on the needs of the children, have them work in pairs to discuss each illustration in turn, before reading the letter that accompanies it. If the group needs more support, discuss and read as a group. More accomplished readers may find the story more humorous, if they read each letter before a close look at its illustration.

• Reread the story, with volunteers reading Toby's and Millie's letters.

Returning to the text

• Provide opportunities for children to return to the text for pleasure.

• Discuss the story: Talk about how letters tell the reader about the narrator's character. How would you describe Toby? How would you describe Claudine and Millie? (Find examples from the text.) How does each character feel about the camping trip? Why? How are Toby and Millie different? Find a part in the story you think is funny. Why is it funny?

• **Features to note in context:**

— setting out a letter; the use of a postscript *(P.S.)*

— contractions: *We're, haven't, it's* etc.

Responding to the text

• Use the story as a model for writing. After plenty of discussion:

— write a letter about a new episode

— rewrite one letter from Claudine's or Millie's point of view

— write a checklist for Claudine's next camping trip

CAMPING CHECKLIST:
check car
repair tent

— Write a letter about a personal incident, trying not to tell everything. Show what really happened in the illustration.

LINKS TO THEMES

ADVENTURE AND FANTASY

Stage 3

Animals Love the Fair
Aunt Jessie
March Along with Me
Mrs. Bold
My Monster Friends

Stage 4

The Boo-dee-roo
Boxes
My House
Papa's Spaghetti
Philippa and the Dragon
When the Moon Was Blue

Stage 5

The Lonely Giant
Lucy Meets a Dragon
The Oogly Gum Chasing Game
Zoe at the Fancy Dress Ball

Stage 6

Crosby Crocodile's Disguise
Magic All Around
The Monster of Mirror Mountain
Pete's Story
Rapunzel
Snow Goes to Town
The Three Magicians
Why the Sea Is Salty

COMMUNITIES

Stage 3

Aunt Jessie
Christmas Shopping
Green Eyes
Mom's Haircut
Mrs. Bold
Sally's Picture
Screech!

Stage 4

The Barnabys' New House
The Fastest Gazelle
My House
Numerals
What's Around the Corner?
Woolly, Woolly

Stage 5

The Beekeeper
Diary of a Honeybee
The Dragon Who Had the Measles
The Hare and the Tortoise
Knit, Knit, Knit, Knit
The Little Girl and Her Beetle
Lucy Meets a Dragon
Matthew's Tantrum
Morning Star
Mr. Pepperpot's Pet
The Oogly Gum Chasing Game
The Skeleton on the Bus
Tommy's Treasure
Zoe at the Fancy Dress Ball

Stage 6

The Best Birthday Present
Bringing the Sea Back Home
The Cabbage Princess
Cass Becomes a Star
Concert Night
The Monster of Mirror Mountain
Now Listen, Stanley
A Prize for Purry
Rosie's House
Scare-Kid
The Three Sillies
Vicky the High Jumper
Yellow Overalls

CREATURES, MONSTERS AND SCARY THINGS

Stage 3

Sally's Picture

Stage 4

The Boo-dee-roo
The Mess Monster
Philippa and the Dragon

Stage 5

The Lonely Giant
Lucy Meets a Dragon
The Oogly Gum Chasing Game
The Tickle-Bugs

Stage 6

The Monster of Mirror Mountain
Pete's Story
Scare-Kid
The Selfish Giant

FAMILY AND FRIENDS

Stage 3

Aunt Jessie
Christmas Shopping
Dad's Bike
Good-Night, Little Brother
Just Like Grandpa
Lilly-Lolly Little-Legs
Mom's Haircut
Monkey's Friends
No Extras
Pancakes for Supper
Scruffy Messed It Up
The Surprise
Talk, Talk, Talk
T.J.'s Tree

Stage 4

The Barnabys' New House
Can You Carry It, Harriet?
Dad Didn't Mind at All
Dad's Bathtime
The Father Who Walked on His Hands
Grandma's Memories
The Mess Monster
Old Friends

What Tommy Did
When I'm Older
The Wobbly Tooth

Stage 5

Alison Wendlebury
Camping with Claudine
Friends Are Forever
Knit, Knit, Knit, Knit
The Lonely Giant
Lucy Meets a Dragon
Matthew's Tantrum
Something Soft for Danny Bear
Souvenirs
The T-shirt Triplets
Zoe at the Fancy Dress Ball

Stage 6

The Best Birthday Present
Bringing the Sea Back Home
The Dragon Who Had the Measles
The Frog Who Thought He Was a Horse
Grandad
Pete's Story
Rosie's House
The Three Sillies
Vicky the High Jumper
The White Horse

FOOD

Stage 3

The Grump
Pancakes for Supper
Secret Soup

Stage 4

The Hungry Chickens
A Lollipop, Please
No Dinner for Sally
Papa's Spaghetti
Percival
Philippa and the Dragon
Waiting

LINKS TO THEMES

Stage 5

The Beekeeper
Diary of a Honeybee
The Pumpkin House

Stage 6

The Cabbage Princess
Why the Sea Is Salty

HUMOR

Stage 3

Aunt Jessie
Buffy's Tricks
Christmas Shopping
The Grump
Mrs. Bold
No Extras
Sally's Picture
Secret Soup

Stage 4

The Boo-dee-roo
Dad Didn't Mind at All
Dad's Bathtime
The Hat Sale
Roll Over
When I'm Older
The Wide-mouthed Frog
Woolly, Woolly

Stage 5

Camping with Claudine
Just for Fun
Look Out for Your Tail
Mr. Pepperpot's Pet
The Skeleton on the Bus

Stage 6

The Cabbage Princess
Rapunzel
Snow Goes to Town
The Three Sillies

LIVING THINGS

Stage 3

At Night
Birds
Green Eyes
Legs
Sleepy Bear
Talk, Talk, Talk
T.J.'s Tree
What Is Bat?
Wrinkles

Stage 4

The Crab at the Bottom of the Sea
Countdown
Dad's Bathtime
The Deer and the Crocodile
The Fastest Gazelle
The Hungry Chickens
In the Garden
Why Elephants Have Long Noses
The Wide-mouthed Frog

Stage 5

The Beekeeper
Cat Concert
Diary of a Honeybee
Friends Are Forever
The Little Girl and Her Beetle
Mr. Pepperpot's Pet
The Smallest Tree
The Tickle-Bugs

Stage 6

The Frog Who Thought He Was a Horse
I Love the Beach
The Little Spider
Misha Disappears
A Prize for Purry
Rabbits
Snow Goes to Town
Tony and the Butterfly

MATHEMATICS

Stage 3

Animals Love the Fair
Bang
Birds
Christmas Shopping
No Extras
The Printing Machine

Stage 4

Boxes
Countdown
The Hungry Chickens
A Lollipop, Please
Numerals
Roll Over

Stage 5

The Beekeeper
Diary of a Honeybee
The Hare and the Tortoise
Just for Fun
The Lonely Giant
Mr. Pepperpot's Pet
The Pumpkin House
The Skeleton on the Bus
The Smallest Tree
Something Soft for Danny Bear
Souvenirs
The T-Shirt Triplets

Stage 6

Bringing the Sea Back Home

ME AND MY FEELINGS

Stage 3

Dad's Bike
The Grump
Just Like Grandpa
Lilly-Lolly Little-Legs
Moonlight

Stage 4

Brave Ben
Daniel

If You're Happy
Just My Luck
Ripeka's Carving
What Tommy Did
What's Around the Corner?
When I'm Older
The Wobbly Tooth

Stage 5

Alison Wendlebury
Camping with Claudine
Friends Are Forever
Lucy Meets a Dragon
Matthew's Tantrum
Tommy's Treasure
Zoe at the Fancy Dress Ball

Stage 6

The Best Birthday Present
Charlie
Concert Night
Crosby Crocodile's Disguise
Grandad
I Love the Beach
Misha Disappears
Now Listen, Stanley
A Prize for Purry
Rosie's House
The Selfish Giant
The Three Magicians
Tony and the Butterfly
The White Horse

MOVEMENT

Stage 3

Animals Love the Fair
BMX Billy
Buffy's Tricks
Dad's Bike
March Along with Me
The Printing Machine

Stage 4

LINKS TO THEMES

Countdown
If You're Happy
Roll Over

Stage 5

The Beekeeper
Diary of a Honeybee
The Hare and the Tortoise
Knit, Knit, Knit, Knit
The Oogly Gum Chasing Game

Stage 6

The Best Birthday Present
Cass Becomes a Star
Clouds
Concert Night
The Little Spider
Pete's Story
Rosie's House
Tony and the Butterfly

MUSIC AND RHYTHM

Stage 3

Bang
Birds
March Along with Me
Riddles

Stage 4

Countdown
If You're Happy
Roll Over

Stage 5

Dogstar
The Little Girl and Her Beetle
The Lonely Giant
Lucy Meets a Dragon
The Oogly Gum Chasing Game

Stage 6

Concert Night

NIGHT

Stage 3

At Night
Good-Night, Little Brother
Moonlight

Stage 4

Brave Ben
The Mess Monster
Roll Over
When the Moon Was Blue

Stage 5

Cat Concert
Lucy Meets a Dragon
The Oogly Gum Chasing Game
Zoe at the Fancy Dress Ball

Stage 6

Concert Night

NONFICTION

Stage 4

Numerals

Stage 5

The Beekeeper
Diary of a Honeybee

Stage 6

Cass Becomes a Star
Clouds
I Love the Beach
Rabbits

PETS

Stage 3

Buffy's Tricks
Green Eyes
The Grump
Scruffy Messed It Up
The Surprise

Stage 4

No Dinner for Sally
Percival
What Tommy Did

Stage 5

Cat Concert
Dogstar
The Little Girl and Her Beetle
Mr. Pepperpot's Pet

Stage 6

Cass Becomes a Star
Misha Disappears
A Prize for Purry
Rosie's House
Vicky the High Jumper

PLAYS

Stage 5

The Two Foolish Cats

Stage 6

The Boy Who Went to the North Wind

PROBLEM-SOLVING

Stage 3

My Monster Friends
Riddles
The Surprise

Stage 4

Boxes
Can You Carry It, Harriet?
Emma's Problem
Numerals

Stage 5

Alison Wendlebury
The Beekeeper
Camping with Claudine
Diary of a Honeybee

Don't Worry
The Hare and the Tortoise
Look Out for Your Tail
Lucy Meets a Dragon
Matthew's Tantrum
The Oogly Gum Chasing Game
The Pumpkin House
Something Soft for Danny Bear
Souvenirs
The Tickle-Bugs
Zoe at the Fancy Dress Ball

Stage 6

The Best Birthday Present
Bringing the Sea Back Home
Crosby Crocodile's Disguise
The Frog Who Thought He Was a Horse
Misha Disappears
Rosie's House
The Selfish Giant
The Three Magicians
The Three Sillies
Vicky the High Jumper
Why the Sea Is Salty
Yellow Overalls

SPECIAL DAYS

Stage 3

Bruno's Birthday
Christmas Shopping
Pancakes for Supper
Rain
Sally's Picture
Sneezes
The Surprise

Stage 4

The Fastest Gazelle
Just My Luck
Mrs. Bold
T.J.'s Tree
The Wobbly Tooth

Stage 5

Lucy Meets a Dragon

Stage 6

The Best Birthday Present
Concert Night
The White Horse

TRADITIONAL

Stage 3

Bang
Birds
Riddles
Sneezes
What Is Bat?

Stage 4

The Crab at the Bottom of the Sea
The Deer and the Crocodile
The Hungry Chickens
If You're Happy
Roll Over
Why Elephants Have Long Noses

Stage 5

The Hare and the Tortoise
He Who Listens
The Two Foolish Cats

Stage 6

The Boy Who Went to the North Wind
Rapunzel
The Selfish Giant
The Three Sillies
Why the Sea Is Salty

WEATHER, SEASONS & SKY

Stage 3

At Night
Moonlight
Mr. Wind
Rain
Sleepy Bear

Stage 4

In the Garden

Stage 5

Camping with Claudine

Morning Star
Something Soft for Danny Bear

Stage 6

The Boy Who Went to the North Wind
Charlie
Clouds

LINKS TO AUTHORS

AUTHOR	STAGE	TITLE	AUTHOR	STAGE	TITLE
R. Grey Armstrong	5	Tommy's Treasure	Margaret Mahy	6	The Three Magicians
Ron Bacon	5	Cat Concert	Judith Marra Scott	6	Tony and the
Margaret Beames	6	Snow Goes to Town			Butterfly
	6	The Little Spider	Graham Meadows	6	Rabbits
Jennifer Beck	5	Souvenirs		6	Cass Becomes a Star
	6	Rapunzel	Ngarangi Naden	5	The Tickle-Bugs
Rhoda Broekhuizen	5	Something Soft for	John Parker	5	Look Out for Your
		Danny Bear			Tail
Celia Burrows	6	Vicky the High	Gwen Pascoe	5	Mr. Pepperpot's Pet
		Jumper		5	The Skeleton on the
Pauline Cartwright	5	Knit, Knit, Knit, Knit			Bus
	5	Don't Worry	Susan Reid	5	Lucy Meets a Dragon
	5	Just For Fun		5	Zoe at the Fancy
	6	Concert Night			Dress Ball
	6	Grandad		6	Rosie's House
	6	I Love the Beach	Janet Slater Redhead	6	A Prize for Purry
	6	Magic All Around	Leanna Traill	5	The Two Foolish Cats
Joy Cowley	6	The White Horse		6	Why the Sea Is Salty
	6	Yellow Overalls		6	The Selfish Giant
	6	The Cabbage Princess	Marcia Vaughan	6	Crosby Crocodile's
Avelyn Davidson	5	He Who Listens			Disguise
	6	The Boy Who Went to		6	Clouds
		the North Wind		6	Scare-Kid
Hazel Edwards	5	The T-Shirt Triplets	Richard Vaughan	6	Charlie
	5	Dogstar	Roger Vaughan Carr	5	The Pumpkin House
Jenny Hessell	6	Now Listen, Stanley		6	The Frog Who
Jan Hill	5	Matthew's Tantrum			Thought He Was a
Janet Hillman	5	The Hare and the			Horse
		Tortoise		6	The Monster of
Nette Hilton	5	The Oogly Gum			Mirror Mountain
		Chasing Game	Edel Wignell	5	The Little Girl and
	5	Alison Wendlebury			Her Beetle
Patricia Johnson	5	The Smallest Tree	Judy Wilford	5	Dom's Handplant
	5	Morning Star	Nelwyn Wright	5	Friends Are Forever
Bill Keir	5	Diary of a Honeybee		6	Misha Disappears
Virginia King	5	Camping with			
		Claudine			
	6	The Best Birthday			
		Present			
	6	Pete's Story			
Carol Krueger	5	The Dragon Who Had			
		the Measles			
Lucy Lawrence	5	The Lonely Giant			
	6	Bringing the Sea Back			
		Home			
	6	The Three Sillies			
Jan Maguiness	5	The Beekeeper			

LINKS TO ILLUSTRATORS

ILLUSTRATOR	STAGE	TITLE
Martin Bailey	6	The Boy Who Went to the North Wind
Virginia Barrett	5	Alison Wendlebury
Robyn Belton	6	Yellow Overalls
Linda Bieniasz (photography)	5	Dom's Handplant
Kevin Burgemeestre	6	Pete's Story
Sandra Cammell	6	Rapunzel
Margie Chellew	6	The Monster of Mirror Mountain
Teresa Culkin-Lawrence	6	Rosie's House
Julie Davey	5	The Pumpkin House
Mary Davy	6	The Scare-Kid
Liz Dodson	5	Tommy's Treasure
Bettina Guthridge	5	Camping with Claudine
Kelvin Hawley	5	Look Out for Your Tail
	6	Why the Sea Is Salty
Lucinda Hunnam	5	The Oogly Gum Chasing Game
John Hurford	6	The Little Spider
	6	The Selfish Giant
Ester Kasepuu	6	Bringing the Sea Back Home
Bill Keir (photography)	5	Diary of a Honeybee
	6	I Love the Beach
Lyn Kriegler	5	Cat Concert
	6	Concert Night
Judy Lambert	5	The Smallest Tree
Marie Low	5	He Who Listens
	6	Grandad
Sarah Matthewson	6	Magic All Around
Marina McAllan	5	Dogstar
	5	The Hare and the Tortoise
	5	Matthew's Tantrum
Ian McNee	5	Don't Worry
Rodney McRae	5	Friends Are Forever
	6	Snow Goes to Town
Graham Meadows (photography)	6	Rabbits
	6	Cass Becomes a Star
Philippa Miles	6	The Three Magicians
Rebecca Pannell	5	Souvenirs
Rita Parkinson	5	Morning Star
Mark Payne	5	Something Soft for Danny Bear
	5	The Skeleton on the Bus
David Pearson	6	The Three Sillies
	6	Vicky the High Jumper
Bryan Pollard	6	Charlie
Margaret Power	5	The T-Shirt Triplets
Trevor Pye	5	The Dragon Who Had the Measles
	6	The Cabbage Princess
Gene Rigney (photography)	5	The Beekeeper
Robert Roennfeldt	5	The Little Girl and Her Beetle
Gregory Rogers	5	Lucy Meets a Dragon
	5	Zoe at the Fancy Dress Ball
Christine Ross	6	Misha Disappears
Ann Skelly	5	Knit, Knit, Knit, Knit
	6	Now Listen, Stanley
Craig Smith	5	The Lonely Giant
	6	The Frog Who Thought He Was a Horse
Manu Smith	6	Tony and the Butterfly
John Tarlton	5	The Tickle-Bugs
	5	The Two Foolish Cats
Dianne Vanderee	5	Mr. Pepperpot's Pet
Mitch Vane	6	The Best Birthday Present
Philip Webb	5	Just For Fun
	6	Crosby Crocodile's Disguise
Elette Wheeler	6	A Prize for Purry
Fraser Williamson	6	The White Horse

INDEX

A

Alison Wendlebury   33

B

The Beekeeper   28
Book Boxes   8, 9

C

Camping with Claudine   45
Cat Concert   25

D

Diary of a Honeybee   29
Dogstar   38
Dom's Handplant   40
Don't Worry   19
The Dragon Who Had the Measles   21

E

Evaluation and Monitoring   9

F

Friends Are Forever   24

G

Glossary of Terms Used   10
Guided Reading   4-7, 8

H

The Hare and the Tortoise   43
He Who Listens   27

I

Independent Reading   4, 8-9

J

Just For Fun   20

K

Knit, Knit, Knit, Knit   14

L

Links to Authors   53
Links to Illustrators 54
Links to Themes   46
The Little Girl and Her Beetle   37
The Lonely Giant   30
Look Out For Your Tail   18
Lucy Meets a Dragon   41

M

Matthew's Tantrum   44
Morning Star   22
Mr. Pepperpot's Pet   34

O

The Oogly Gum Chasing Game   31

P

The Pumpkin House   32

S

Selecting texts for Guided Reading   7
The Skeleton on the Bus   39
The Smallest Tree   23
Something Soft for Danny Bear   35
Souvenirs   15
A suggested teaching sequence
for Guided Reading   6-7

T

The Tickle-Bugs   16
Tommy's Treasure   17
The T-Shirt Triplets   36
The Two Foolish Cats   26

Z

Zoe at the Fancy Dress Ball   42

NOTES